GW00656243

The Answer Is In You

Find it – in 9 clear steps

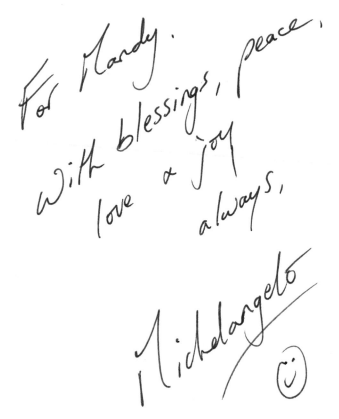

For Mandy.
With blessings, peace,
love & joy
always,

Michelangelo :)

The Answer Is In You

Find it – in 9 clear steps

Michelangelo Raiano

youcanbeyourself.com

Printed in the UK for MRT Response
www.mrtresponse.com

This publication is printed on FSC-certified and totally
chlorine-free paper.

FSC (the Forest Stewardship Council) is an international
network to promote responsible management of the
world's forests.

Dedicated to my father
Guido Raiano

If you are aware of a part of yourself,
or your life, that you know could be
or should be better -

and you may have the power
to do something about it
but choose not to -

then you are already in danger.

'In danger of what?' I hear you ask.

In danger of losing yourself!

The danger of denying a part of you real
expression, real freedom in life and real
benefit -

the consequences of which are immeasurable.

Introduction

We all want to live a better life and we all have some part of ourselves, or our life, we would like to improve, unless of course *we have already reached perfection!*

However, how many of us are truly prepared to do anything about it? And if we do, how is it that most of us give up at the first hurdle?

There are, no doubt, many reasons for this.

But suppose there were a way that could show us that *yes*, we can influence the outcome of events to be in line with our highest ideals and dreams, that we *can* have what we desire, that we are meant to have it, and that it is ours for the claiming simply by applying some basic principles in life, some basic Laws of Nature.

Then would it not be a worthwhile pursuit, for our betterment, our time on the planet and the rest of the world, to explore and make use of such Natural Laws?

WARNING

This book has the power to help you get the
life of your dreams,

however...

If you do not wish to embark on a journey of self-improvement, self-development and self-discovery, or if you are not prepared to let down your barriers and look honestly at yourself with open eyes *regardless of what you may see there;*

nor be willing to make whatever personal sacrifices may be necessary, with the risk that some things may even appear worse in the short term before they seem to settle into something better in the longer term, in order to move closer to your ideal;

then simply close this book now, put it back on the shelf or give it to somebody else...

or if you have reached perfection already!

Phew!

I'm so glad you're still holding this book and have chosen to read on.

*"In each life there comes
at least one moment which,
if recognized and seized,
transforms the course of that life
forever"*

Ralph Blum

This,

is

that moment.

Let us begin…

I will guide you through nine steps that will bring clarity and direction to improve or change anything or any situation in your life.

These nine steps will help you go through the process of change, find out what you really want, the direction you need to go in and all the steps necessary to make the changes as quickly as possible.

I don't tell you or teach you anything.

I simply guide you through the nine steps.

You do everything else.

The answers *you* are looking for will come out of you.

All the answers you are looking for are inside you right now.

All I am doing is giving you the tools to get those answers out.

It's as simple as that.

The only requirements…

are that you recognize an area of unhappiness
in your life -
something you know deep down should be
better -
and that you are open to change it.

Do you recognize that area?

All the events you are about to read that led to the nine step process being created, and the ways in which it materialized, are completely true.

Let me share with you how it all happened...

Chapter 1

I confess

I had been in a mess most of my life but didn't want to see it.

Of course, I was able to hide it well, except to those closest to me, my loved ones, who could see another side of me. It was that part of me that struggled to really get anywhere in life. I call it my shadow side, the shadow side of my otherwise quite positive and optimistic personality. Sure, I've had some good times, some successes but I wasn't able to sustain them or manifest them at will.

What was it that I struggled with for so long, *in fact,* the last 30 years of my life?

First of all I struggled with finding my right direction. I say "struggled" because at times I did have it, only to see it quickly leave me again, sometimes for long periods at a time. I also struggled with getting motivated in the first place and with staying on track once I was motivated. Then, when I did manage to see my goals clearly, I'd struggle to make them happen and with the changes that I needed to make as well. On top of all that, I had dark bouts of depression and crippling fear. Then I would have to battle with my energy, my deflation and my spirits to get myself in the right frame of mind just to start again!

Sometimes I managed, perhaps after a few months, sometimes even years, to pick up where I had left off. More often than not I kept myself really busy because I could always find things to distract myself from what I really wished to do.

I was even like this as a schoolboy. At that time I just blamed it on school being boring and where I lived being boring, looking at everything else but myself. I found it hard to focus my mind and study well. In my free time I always had lots of ideas but could never direct myself to get anything done. And so it continued all through my teenage years and as an adult; nothing changed much except the scenery.

I would have my good intentions. Some time ago I decided to write a book about health. I had a good background in natural health care and as I no longer wished to work as a therapist I still wanted to make use of my knowledge and experience.

I told everyone I was doing this and doing that and working on my goal, but really what I meant by that was that I'd plan to start the day early and be at my desk for 9 o'clock. So I would get up early and then instantly think 'Hey I'm up nice and early. Why don't I go for a nice morning walk? I have the time, it's only 7 o'clock. I love going for walks especially so early in the morning when the air is fresh and everything is so peaceful'. I would wander back about an hour later, look at my desk and by then, of course, be hungry and thirsty so I would fix myself some breakfast.

As I was eating I would think how well I was doing - by then it was still only 8.30a.m. 'I've got lots of time before I need to be at my desk' I would say to myself. So I'd read the papers a little. Then when it was almost 9 o'clock I would think 'OK, better get ready to start work' when all of a sudden, the postman would arrive and deliver a few letters. Well of course I had to check my mail, oh and one was a bill and it seemed to be for more than I expected that month. 'I'd better check my finances'.

Before I knew it, it was 10 a.m. already. So I sat at my desk but then I'd think 'I'd better just check my e-mails before I start as I'm waiting to hear from a friend'. I would eventually get started at about 11.30a.m. - by "started" I mean making a faint attempt, shuffling a few bits of paper around and then realize it was almost lunchtime, so I would have to stop and prepare some lunch…

you can imagine the rest.

This is how it continued for many months. Ok I'll be honest, for several years, about two or three to be exact. And I feel shame about it. It wasn't only my total lack of time management and will power each day that caused me to get nowhere for a long time, I could just as easily distract myself with things that felt good to me too, such as a relationship!

The following three years I had a lovely, deep and meaningful relationship with a wonderful lady. The distractions came thick and fast, mostly in the form of wanting to live with her. So I uprooted, moved to another part of the country and then realized I needed to pay my way so I spent a few months looking for a job. I managed to find one I liked but after two months my partner was relocated so I left the job, we moved house, settled in and I looked for another job. That all took about another six months. We got settled, I found a job but a few months later we decided to buy a house instead of renting our current place. We found a nice house in another town, but it needed some work doing, etc. etc.

All in all, that cost me another three years. Not because the relationship wasn't good and that it didn't enrich my life in many ways; it was very good and did enrich me a lot. It was that all those events took time away from something deep down within me that needed attention and therefore should have been my number one priority. As I continued to prioritise everything else, I grew unhappier and more unfulfilled by the week to the point that I felt I was so off track in my life that my relationship suffered as a result. Perhaps something similar also had a part to play in the ending of my marriage some years previously.

I'd so easily allow myself to get distracted by this little job here, this little relationship there, only to find another year *or three* had passed and I was no closer to getting back on track. I finally understood what was meant by the words *"The road to hell is paved with good intention"*. I was deflated again, this time more than ever.

I reached absolute rock bottom when in the space of about six months my long term relationship ended, *no surprise,* my children moved five thousand miles away with their mum to start a new life abroad, I had to leave my job, move house, move town, start a new full time job which promised me everything and delivered less and less each week, till my hours ended up at just seven hours one week and the promises - *were never delivered!*

Well, I guess you can imagine what I was going through and how I felt. It was certainly a period of huge changes in my life. Everything was ending, it felt like death all around me and at the time I couldn't see what it all meant and why it had to happen, especially to me! I was always told that *"Life begins at 40"* but for me, it was ending, ending big time! The only thing that kept me going, without completely falling apart, was a little voice deep within me which kept whispering…

'Everything is ending so something greater can come'

but I didn't have a clue what!

Luckily though, I have always believed that good things can come out of apparently negative situations, as I have often witnessed it to be true, so I decided to go with my inner voice on this, my intuition.

I did get depressed at times, wondered where I went wrong in my life, how on earth I ended up here at this place at forty years of age when most people seemed to be established in good careers by this time with good money coming in, pensions lined up, holidays and new cars; with good, stable relationships, home and social life.

Apart from the odd down period, on the whole, I managed to keep fairly positive throughout that time. I'll let you know how in a few moments. However, when the down periods came they were the blackest, darkest and most frightening hell holes I had ever experienced. I later discovered that they were also some of the best things to ever happen to me. In those periods some amazing miracles happened. But I'll also share that with you later.

That was where I had arrived at the end of my 40th year.

So how did I change my reality?

As I have already mentioned, I had been working on a book idea for a number of years and decided to continue with this because it seemed as though it was all I had left. It was the one area that I still had some control over and could do something about. So that was a positive. Then I started working on my self, on picking up all the pieces, putting *me* back together in a way that somehow would make sense.

The first thing I looked at was how I could start taking care of myself. I thought about the things that nurtured me, the things that made me feel good. I'd just been through the year from hell so I knew I deserved to be pampered a little to help *"my recovery"* and as there was no one else to do it, I decided to do it myself.

I made a list of the things that I knew made me feel good, such as spending time in nature, seeing funny or uplifting films, keeping in touch with friends, daily exercise, learning guitar, going to live music events. Then I made a plan of the week and scheduled all these activities into my weekly routine. It felt good! I had a plan that I could work on so that at least I would begin feeling more positive and optimistic again, as I knew those activities would make me feel better. I confess I didn't manage to stick to it rigidly or do everything as I'd planned. However, because my attention was focusing on those things that nurtured me, even if I only managed to exercise once one week, it was a start and did make me feel better.

That worked, so I decided the next step would be to tackle all the unfinished jobs that were always on my mind and therefore blocking my vision of the way forward. These were things like getting my environment comfortable and orderly. I'd just moved house, spent time grieving over my losses, started new work and hadn't had time to unpack properly, put things in their rightful place or to throw out and recycle anything that was no longer of use to me. So I did it and gave my house a thorough "spring clean" which also felt very good.

Within two weeks I was starting to feel significantly better.

That was the beginning, and I thought I'd finally cracked it, but what came to me over the coming weeks was what really turned my life around and later became…

"The Answer Is In You
Find it – in 9 Clear Steps"

Chapter 2

This was, I felt, a very good start and then Christmas arrived. I took a break for a few weeks, decided to visit my mother and a few friends around the country as I thought this would be a much better option than just staying at home on my own, with the danger of getting depressed without my children around.

I enjoyed a very peaceful, pleasant and relaxing time. Even the New Year began very nicely but back at home I awoke in my bed on the second of January when, all of a sudden, it hit me! Thoughts of everything I needed to do and achieve that year came flooding into my mind, everything I'd successfully managed to forget about over the holiday period. I was doing so well just before the break but taking that time off made me completely lose the flow and I felt I was back at square one again, this time more overwhelmed than ever.

There were the practical things like earning a decent living - remember that my current job wasn't providing anywhere near enough hours of work to cover my living expenses. I also wasn't happy with the area I was living in and my house was too small. I had no social life and no money for it either. There were still unfinished jobs around the house, the garden was overgrown, my washing machine was leaking and the car needed fixing. I thought to myself 'Some start to the year buddy!'

So what happened?

Well the first thing I did…

was get thoroughly depressed.

Oh yes, it completely overshadowed me and kept me in a state of worry, hopelessness and despair for most of that first week. I had so much to do I didn't know where to begin, besides which I was in such a confused and stressed emotional state that I found it hard to see the next step clearly anyway. When I did manage to decide on something, by the next day *and sometimes later on the same day*, I would change my mind completely and then it would change again to something else that I thought would be the next best step for me.

This carried on for days but it really worried me. I had lost practically all my remaining self-confidence, any faith in myself or my life and was starting to think that I would lose the plot completely and never get control of my life ever again. That scared me, *a lot* - my greatest fears were beginning to come true. I kept thinking that all that was drilled into me as a child - that my choices were no good and that I wasn't good at anything - was perhaps true. After all, I was incapable of being content in a job for more than a couple of years, incapable of supporting my family properly, incapable of holding any lasting relationship together.

It was a mess, *I was in a mess.* If I had allowed this to continue my life would have fallen apart for sure.

"In every crisis there is danger *and* opportunity"

"Sink or swim" is another well known phrase...

but what do you do when you've sunk already?

I needed help and an answer fast, only divine help and divine answers could save me now.

Can you hear the Angels singing, as they do whenever there is a divine revelation?

This was one of those moments, one that I will never forget.

I was already using a journal for writing my own personal daily experiences, thoughts and reflections. Keeping a journal is an excellent tool that when used regularly helps maintain a sense of flow, connection and peacefulness. However, during this crisis the journal just wasn't effective enough.

I was feeling really emotional and frustrated so I would just scribble my thoughts and feelings on big pieces of paper and throw them on the floor. This was just to help get my emotions out, instead of having them continually swimming around in my head and my whole being.

It was very helpful, but not only that. The more I continued with it the more I realized that once the initial emotion was out, something unusual was starting to happen. It was as though wisdom was beginning to weave itself into the words that followed the outbursts.

Sometimes my outbursts would take the form of a question. What surprised me was that no sooner had I completed writing the question, sometimes as I was still writing it, the answers would simply pop into my head and not just any old answers but genuinely constructive answers that made good sense! At the time some of the answers didn't make complete sense to me, and to my analytical mind appeared too grand or unrealistic to follow, but none the less I would write down what came to me.

<u>Intuition:</u> immediate understanding by the mind, or a sense, without reasoning; *immediate insight.*

I put all this down to my intuition. It was working well and I was listening to it well.

It was as though I was having a conversation with someone right there. It could have been my Higher Self, my Spirit Guide, my Guardian Angel, God, or just plain old intuition. Perhaps it's all the same thing at the end of the day, but we'll save that discussion for another book.

The way I understand it now…

was that I had to get out of my "mind".

You know, not the conscious, in the moment, in the *now*, very present mind which brings complete peace and a sense of oneness with all that is; but the mind that is constantly getting in the way, constantly chattering away, mostly about nothing of any importance at all, yet has the power to overshadow who we really are most of the time and prevents us from experiencing any real peace - *that mind!*

There was just so much going on in that little head of mine, so much turmoil, that the normal methods for quietening the mind that I usually used were not working at all at that time. These included: meditation, writing my journal, exercise, talking with friends and walking in nature. Nothing was effective against the brutal storm within me. Finally, in complete desperation and anguish I was scribbling frantically in big writing, on big pieces of paper, everything that was concerning me, worrying me and causing such huge pain at that time.

First page:

'I've had enough of this, I don't want it anymore!'

On the second page I wrote:

'What is it you want?'

I just stared at this for quite some time and pondered its meaning. 'What did I want?' I asked myself. I had never been asked that question before and I had certainly never asked it to myself. It surprised me how such a simple, brief question could throw me. After a while some ideas started to form so I wrote them underneath the question, then pinned it to the wardrobe door that was right next to my bed and always in view.

It read:

'To have the chance to live abroad, or in the UK, in a beautiful place in nature, near gorgeous towns, or all of it.
To have financial self-sufficiency through publishing or my own successful business which can be based anywhere, or both.
To have time, fun, lots of money and freedom in work.
To always be in credit with all my needs easily covered.'

I was sitting in bed, just looking at the words I had pinned up, thinking how far removed my current situation was from this ideal I had just envisaged and which really felt right. I felt bad at my current reality, felt I was in such chaos and confusion in myself that I must have been contributing to the chaos and confusion on the planet, instead of what I wished to see: peace, harmony, prosperity, truthfulness, love and joy - everything I was lacking. You see, we can all think we really want world peace but have we achieved that in our own little lives yet, in our own tiny corner of the globe? If we were all able to put things right in ourselves, thereby creating peace within ourselves, within our family and home, within our circle of influence, would we not instantly have world peace?

This is how we are all responsible for what we see outside of ourselves as well as inside.

I took another page and wrote:

'Forgive me, I have been in a mess for such a long time and especially the last few days with the possibility of jeopardizing what I wish to become. I have contributed to the disharmony, chaos and confusion on the planet instead of always being a provider of peace, light, harmony and joy, for that I am truly sorry. Can I put all this right now and never allow myself to create this ever again?'

Then the thought came to write down what I would like to see happen. I knew I couldn't change the past but there was time to affect the future as it still hadn't arrived at that point.

'I choose to focus myself wholeheartedly every day. I choose not to cause stress to myself or anyone else. I choose to not be a burden to myself, others or society. Therefore, I choose:
To be an instrument of peace, light, care and compassion always.
To focus myself and my energies every day to unfolding the best I can be.
To support myself properly otherwise I continue to cause worry to family members and that's not good enough for me.
To find the right career direction that I may only radiate satisfaction, joy, fulfilment, trust and confidence in life.
To always use my time really well. Thank you.'

This continued for several days, this looking at myself and what I really wanted. I did a lot of soul searching and soul talking in my journal, in fact not just in my journal. Whenever I was alone I would ask my inner self questions about anything that was on my mind, then I would centre my attention and listen carefully for an answer. The answers came every time! The times I didn't *hear* the answer were when I had a lot of emotions flying around my system such as when I was angry about something or depressed and when I hadn't quietened my mind or centred it away from outside distractions. Like anything else, it became easier the more I did it.

I grew curious. The process had been working so well for some time now that I felt I could ask about anything and get an answer. I asked…

'Are you my Angel, my *Guardian* Angel?'
The answer came:
'Yes'.
I thought WOW!
I then asked:
'Have you always been with me and is it only you?'
The response was:

'Other Angels and Spirit Guides come from time to time but I have always been with you'.

I asked for a name and it was given me. This I was told to keep private.

I became overwhelmed with tears and emotion, which always happens whenever my soul is touched, and all my pain just melted away. When this was happening it felt as though my room was filled with light and lightness, and that I was enveloped in the most exquisite gentleness, care and love imaginable. Since that day I have directed my questions directly to my Angel, by name, and he always responds reassuringly with:
'I am here'.

The more I considered what I would like to see happen in my life, tackling the biggest issues first, the more clarity kept coming through. As I wrote answers down it felt as though the new me was starting to take form before my very eyes. It was great! With each new page and each new insight I was feeling increasingly more clear and powerful. My heavy desperate and dark depression was lifting - *not just lifting;*

it was being blasted out at a phenomenal rate just like the sun breaking through clouds after a huge storm, clearing them all away to restore light and beauty again. This is how all this was making me feel. It was brilliant and showed no sign of stopping.

Miracles were beginning to happen.

Chapter 3

That was the start of the new me becoming reality. What quickly followed helped clarify the final steps I would need to take, the changes I would have to go through and exactly what I had to do to bring it all about.

I did have several relapses where I seemed to lose sight of everything that I had been visualizing and wanting. This I realized later was mostly due to self-doubt, doubting that I could do it and doubting that I was worthy enough to have it anyway. I feel this may have come from years of past conditioning from others and also myself. Yes, I lacked faith and belief in myself and so, of course, I attracted it from others too. It was one of the worst realizations I ever had to face up to about myself. I thought I was generally confident but it was only in some areas of my life; I was fairly sociable and could be comfortable in new situations, however in other areas confidence completely eluded me.

So there I was: I had been blessed with divine insight and inspiration, I was fired up, energized and ready to go, when suddenly I was stopped dead in my tracks, gripped by a terrible demonic force and completely unable to move forward. I could see the new me, my new life very clearly, it was there in front of me. I knew it was for me, but now it seemed so far out of reach because I was so held back by...

NO - not the wrong job anymore, NO - not the wrong relationship anymore, NO - not all the distractions I usually had, NO - not even money. It was *fear* - nothing more, nothing less. *Fear* from my lack of self-belief, lack of self worth.

'Oh no!' I thought 'It's still with me after all these years, ready as ever to rear its ugly head the moment I want to really do something for me. How could this be happening to me now, when I least need it?'

Divine help was needed again but this time I was so angry at my life, my weakness, myself that I couldn't possibly hear my inner voice or Angel now. I was raging. I shouted out to the universe and to the weaker me 'I DO DESERVE MY NEW LIFE AND WHAT'S MORE IT'S WELL OVERDUE!' *It continued...* 'I am changing this current reality which has been with me for so many years, caused me to lose my loved ones on many occasions and kept me in limiting beliefs and experiences. Staying the same, in this reality, for one more day is a sentence worse than hell! It's been keeping me small-minded and is no longer an option. I've had it with part time jobs, with no real prospects and not managing to get by so I am choosing to end this reality *today*, here and now! I choose *never* and I mean NEVER to allow myself to live like this again.'

I put it all in writing in my journal so I would never forget it. I was still fuming and more quickly followed: 'I am doing it *now*, not tomorrow or next week, NOW! I do it for *me*, for my children, my family, friends, all who love me, know me and for the rest of the world. Oh, I pledge to follow through on this, no matter what, until the desired result is achieved. I pledge to face whatever is thrown at me, the fears, the discomfort and to simply carry on until I get what I want and deserve.'

The war was on. I felt like a warrior about to enter battle. Of course I felt some fear of war and was somewhat apprehensive, it was only natural. Even great warriors with immense courage and strength must feel this just before battle, I thought. I then wrote: 'I centre myself and call on COURAGE to assist me in these dark hours to face what has to be faced and only I can do for myself, boldly, courageously, honourably, with dignity and truth as my strength. Others have gone before on this treacherous journey. Many have turned back and settled for safety, safe lives, safe jobs, *but at a price*. I choose to fight! I choose my freedom, regardless of the outcome. I will invest *all* my energy to this urgent situation. During a war, having courage, strength, discipline and alertness – these things take priority. When I have faced these fears and fought like a true Spiritual Warrior, I will have mastered vitally important lessons for growth. I will then be able to help many more souls when they are ready to face their demons as there is no doubt that many wonderful guides and souls are assisting me right now and will be there with me all the way. I will be strong, *I am strong!* I will be courageous, *I am courageous!* I am supported on all sides because the timing is right for me to walk this journey now. I listen to my inner voice constantly.'

What followed that moment changed the course of my life forever.

I was in pain; I was in my darkest night of the soul ever. I had stripped away at every façade, every hope, everything I'd held dear, even every fear, everything that I had in my life until that day. I was left beaten and bare. Yet I stood up and stated to the universe 'I am ready to fight, with every scrap of energy I have left, for the future of my dreams and I'm not leaving till I get it!'

Then, that moment, I felt I was granted what I can only describe as a vision, a revelation, the bigger picture of who I really am and my purpose for being here. I felt I had received glimpses of it occasionally in my life before that day, not enough to really believe it, but now here it was in all its glory. It was as though, momentarily, I had escaped my limited human-ness and was able to stand back and witness a much larger reality of my being. Of course, I wrote it all down in my journal.

'The physical boundaries of my everyday world started melting away, until I stood alone in an unending ocean of light, silence and power. Fear did not exist, nor any doubt - only certainty, truth, strength. I felt at one with the whole universe, that all was perfect, has always been and always will be. I became aware of the cosmic status each one of us has and the importance of our place in this beautiful universe.'

The following words filled my awareness:

'I fear nothing.
I am brave.
I am courageous.
I am strength.
I am compassion.
I am joy.
I am peace.

I am oneness.

I am love.

All my thoughts, words and actions uphold who I truly am.'

As my normal physical world emerged again, I gradually became aware of my familiar surroundings - *only I felt changed*. I felt infused with an experience and a truth that we are all worthy of the absolute best, for without our participation in this whole cosmic dance, the universe and life would not be complete.

I never doubted myself again after that day.

With that, the final steps to change my reality had been given me...

and now here they are for you

Chapter 4

The

9

Steps

Instructions

To really get the most from this book and from this nine step process, having the right beginning is very important. Also, following the order of the steps as they are presented and resisting the temptation to rush ahead is vital.

It is better not to look at and move on to subsequent steps, until the current step is completed to your satisfaction.

Patience and a steady approach will bring you the maximum and best results from this book.

These nine steps are a journey, your personal journey of self-improvement, growth and discovery. So just like any other journey, it is undertaken simply by putting one small step in front of the other, one step at a time until the destination is reached.

And what is that destination?

It is that place of total clarity, peace, power and confidence in any situation of your choice. You will know yourself *and be living it!*

The first step alone has the power to start transforming your current reality. However, the subsequent steps build on the first and support and strengthen each other so that you are not just empowered by one thing, *but by nine*. It's a very powerful process and will bring you to more of your true self.

In fact, just by having gone through Step 1, you may find that the procedure of aiming to improve, clarify or change a situation will start to happen of its own accord, without having to do anything and without having to involve others. The simple act of visualizing the outcome you really want to see sets the cosmic ball in motion. You're informing the Universe what outcome you really want and, in all its abundance and infinite power, it starts doing what it does best: rearranging physical matter to bring you the reality you wish to see. People, places, things, situations will all start to alter in some way to better accommodate the new you and your new idea about yourself, sometimes in ways we never could expect. New opportunities may also start gravitating towards you, effortlessly. Look out for that one; it's called "synchronicity".

I feel a little quantum physics coming on here...

don't worry; it's all in simple English.

At one time scientists believed the atom to be the smallest and most fundamental part of the physical universe. Modern science has now realized that underlying the atom, at much subtler levels of creation, there are even more fundamental forces at work such as the activity of "subatomic particles" which are not solid but simply fluctuations of energy and intelligence. Therefore, you, me, this chair, this book, this table, this building, in fact everything we take for granted as solid is, at its most basic level of existence, not solid at all but pure ENERGY, waves of energy.

This energy fluctuates in an infinite number of ways and frequencies to create the infinite variety that we see in the world around us and in the greater universe. All these fluctuations exist in a big soup of nothingness all the time, but they only exist there as a possibility. They are not in concrete form, yet, from the big soup – known as the quantum field – absolutely anything is possible. Ever watched any nature programmes and just been amazed at the diversity of it all? Did you know that no two snowflakes are identical and, more importantly, no two moments are the same either?

Each moment of our life is unique, a unique event in time and space, and cannot be duplicated if we tried. Each moment is so precious it's like a gift.

Is that why this moment is called the present?

"To see the world in a grain of sand
and heaven in a wild flower,
hold infinity in the palm of your hand
and eternity in an hour"

William Blake

Have you ever wondered where your thoughts come from?

If everything in the whole universe comes from this basic fundamental field of energy and intelligence then we must do also, but then don't our thoughts too? Remember, at the most basic level nothing is solid. And if it's not solid, what is it then? It's non-physical. Does that mean it could be of spirit or consciousness, a non-physical reality of energy, intelligence and infinite possibility at the basis of the physical world, yet with the power and ability to orchestrate the whole thing with absolute magnificent simplicity and perfection?

If so, what is a thought? It is an impulse of energy and, because it has direction, it is also intelligent. Therefore thought is also simply an energy and intelligence that comes from the field of all possibilities inside us…

and outside us too! If it is at the basis of everything, it must also be everywhere, holding everything together.

Why am I telling you all this?

The reason is that you may start, in case you don't already, to believe that *anything* is possible and *nothing* is impossible. Also that, by our thoughts alone, we can create any reality we wish to see in our life, just as almighty Nature changes and creates whatever it wants *all the time*.

> *"You are created in*
> *the image and likeness of God"*
> The Bible

In fact, the most fascinating thing I find about quantum physics is that the result that comes out of experiments on investigations into the quantum field is affected by whoever is observing. In other words, the thoughts of the experimenter create an *effect* at this most subtle level and, when his or her attention is taken away, the effect disappears also. At this most basic level of reality, we are interconnected with everything else. All creation is composed of nothing but waves of energy fluctuating and interacting with each other. Nothing is separate from anything or anyone else -

WE ARE ONE.

This book will give you the tools to make the universe work for you.

Or is it…

make you work with the universe?

Enjoy

Step 1

Do you have time to begin this process now?

If your answer is no, then just close the book and come back to this page when you are ready. It is not absolutely necessary to do all the steps at once and certainly, with larger life issues, the process could take weeks or even months. Therefore, take a break whenever you need to. Simply pick up where you left off when you are ready to continue.

If you are ready now, the first thing to do is to get some paper; I like to use an A4 pad and a pen. It is important to write everything down.

You have paper and something to write with?

Good, we can begin.

First of all, bring to your awareness one issue, or area of your life, that you are unhappy with and would like to improve, bring clarity to or change. You now know you are going to address it.

You will need to close your eyes for a few moments to settle and collect yourself. When you have closed the eyes, breathe in slowly through your nose. Breathe fully and deeply using the whole of your lungs. Then, breathe out naturally through the mouth. Do this a few times. As you breathe in observe your energies being drawn in to you, and as you are breathing out observe all stress and tension leaving you. When you have done this a few times you may sit there for a little while longer just enjoying that settled state allowing the breathing to be however it wishes.

You may do that now.

When you have relaxed yourself in this way, take your first sheet of paper. In one corner at the top write "Step 1" and at the top of the page write the following heading:

"What is my ideal outcome with regards to this situation?"

Under this heading write everything you would prefer to see happen with this situation or issue. In other words, if absolutely anything were possible and there were no obstacles, write down what your ideal outcome would be with regards to yourself and others that it may affect, bearing in mind, if other people are involved, that you can not change others, only yourself.

For example, when I was doing this for myself with regards to the issue of no longer enjoying where I was living, I began to visualize an ideal place where I would feel more at home and that would best suit me bringing me all the things I enjoy, thereby making me feel happy and nourished.

I came up with:

'I would like to live in a beautiful place with lots of space and amidst nature with magnificent views including the stars at night and expansive sunrises

and sunsets. I'd like a beautiful traditional house or a wooden eco-house, with a nice log fire for cosy winters. It will be near the sea in an elevated position with sea views but also with lots of greenery, trees and hills close by. It will have spacious rooms with high ceilings, be close to a town but far enough away for me to feel I'm surrounded by nature and on a bus route for my mother to visit. Ideally it will be warm and balmy most of the time, sunny and pleasant with lots of birds and flowers around. I would like to feel really at home where I live and enjoy everything about it - the place, the town, the air, the scenery, the people, the vibes. It must have a buzz; it will feel alive, makes me feel that way too and there will be no language problem. Also, it will have a good balance of interesting and like-minded people around who are open, warm and spiritually aware for stimulating conversations, with visitors coming and going as in a tourist town or exciting place of interest.'

I could have just written *'I just want to live somewhere better'*, but that's not really applying myself at all is it? And it expresses nothing to myself or, more importantly, to the Universe about what I really want because I can't even be bothered to see it myself. What a total waste of time! You must visualize it, imagine it, *dream it.*

If it helps, feel free to close the eyes again for a few moments and at any other time you need to connect with yourself.

Now write down everything you would like to see come to pass. Don't think about it or analyse what comes to you or wonder how you're going to do it at this stage; that will all come later. For now simply write the first things that literally pop into your head with regards to your issue. Write down as many things as possible that come to mind, in as much detail as possible, in other words, everything about it. Don't stop to think, simply be open. GO!

When you have written as much as you can for now, more ideas will probably come to you later, simply re-read what you have written.

How does it make you feel?

If you have done the process well, when you look back at what you've visualized for yourself as the desired outcome you wish to see, you may feel a number of things. You may feel calmer, more peaceful, more powerful, energized, clearer, more resolute, happier, or have a feeling of well-being.

If you feel the same as before then I suggest you throw that page away, close your eyes and this time lie down on your bed for a much longer period. Do not get up until you've connected with the real you and visualized something better for yourself using your basic childlike, innocent imagination. I know, you may not have used that for a very long time but go on, give it a go, I'm sure you will surprise yourself!

If after reading what you have written you do feel any of the above, or even more, then you are ready to proceed onto Step 2.

Step 2

Take another sheet of paper. In one corner at the top write "Step 2" and as the heading write:

"What would happen if everything just stayed the same?"

Now think about everything staying just as it is. If you continued doing things in the same way for the rest of your life with regards to your issue, what would you continue to see? If nothing changed, what would continue to happen? How would that make you feel? How would that affect you? How would that affect your family and others who care about you?

Visualize that now and write it all down, as much as comes to mind and again in as much detail as possible.

When you have written as much as you can, simply re-read what you have written.

How does hearing and seeing all this make you feel?

If you have done the process well, when you look back at what you've visualized for yourself as the outcome if everything just stayed the same, you may feel a number of things. You could feel angry, disappointed, frustrated, let down, sad, lost.

Just stay with that for a few moments longer and continue to feel it.

"If we always do the same things, we'll always get the same results"

You are now ready to proceed onto Step 3.

Step 3

Take another sheet of paper. In one corner at the top write "Step 3" then go back to your first page, Step 1, and write "OUTCOME 1" somewhere near the heading.

Go back to Step 2 and write "OUTCOME 2" somewhere near the heading. Good, now come back to Step 3 and decide which outcome you really prefer to see happen in your life and write:

"From this day forth…"

then in big writing, filling the whole page, write:

"I choose OUTCOME _____ as my reality!"

whilst remembering, of course, to fill in the number of the outcome *you* really choose from today.

Does that feel good, empowering?

Are you beginning to feel that there is light at the end of the tunnel and that anything, actually, just might be possible?

If your answer is yes, then feel free to proceed onto Step 4.

If not and maybe you are still unsure…

re-read Step 1, do not rush, just take your time and allow what you have written to sink in. Then re-read Step 2, again taking your time and allowing yourself to feel fully what you have written. Continue doing this, re-reading Step 1 and then Step 2, until you can feel and see a definite contrast between the two steps, until you feel a clear conviction about the outcome you do prefer.

"Sometimes it gets to the point that the discomfort of staying the same becomes more than the discomfort of facing fears and making changes"

If, after doing the above exercise, you are still struggling with the first few steps then let me suggest you read the first two pages of chapter six which begin just after the introductory paragraph. Those first few pages describe three very useful and effective tools that can greatly assist in getting clear.

Only when this step is completed with certainty may you continue onto Step 4 otherwise the subsequent steps will be ineffective.

Take as long as you need, it's OK. The important things in life can never be rushed.

Step 4

Well done! You are beginning to make excellent progress.

Take another sheet of paper. In one corner at the top write "Step 4" then as the heading write:

"What changes can I make from NOW to ensure I get OUTCOME 1 as my reality?"

There are many things you can do now to get your life, or particular issue, more in line with your ideal. Write down everything that comes to mind. Again don't analyse what comes to you or wonder how you're going to do it at this stage; that will all come later. For now simply write down everything that comes to you. Write down as many things as possible that you know you could do and don't stop to think; simply be open. Two minutes starting now, GO!

Actually, take longer if you need and if you're having lots of ideas.

When you are satisfied with your list, you may proceed to Step 5.

Step 5

The purpose of this next step is to get completely clear what the goals are and *why*.

Take the next sheet of paper. In a corner at the top write "Step 5" then as the heading write, you guessed it:

"Getting completely clear - what are the goals and why?"

A lot of ideas may have come up, some of which may not have been completely relevant, so now is the time to go over that previous step to highlight and list the main points that arose.

This step may be more applicable when working on larger issues but, none the less, it is still a useful step even if only to review what just came up in Step 4.

So go over everything you wrote in Step 4 and now on this page write the key goals down BUT, add the reason *why* after each one.

For example, with regard to my ideal house idea, a key goal would be to start researching and considering different areas around this country or abroad. The reasons *why* may be to keep my dream alive and to begin moving in my desired direction without delay, taking whatever little steps I can take each day.

This step helps to get really specific, to understand the benefits that will come from it and to add more energy to those goals.

So let's do that now.

When you are satisfied with your list, you may proceed to Step 6.

Step 6

Take the next sheet of paper. In a corner at the top write "Step 6" then as the heading write:

"Affirmations to Empower"

Affirmations are statements, statements of intent. They are like formal declarations to the whole universe. They assert an idea strongly and they state it as though it's already a fact.

Having a vague thought about doing something is like a tap dripping. Yes, the idea (or water) is coming out but it's so pathetically weak and slow it's not worth bothering with. Having a clear intention is like a good shower where the water comes out quite forcefully. However, having a clear vision backed by affirmations is like giving your desire the power of Niagara Falls!

So what are affirmations and how do you do them properly?

As we have said already, they are statements and really work when they are stated in the present tense as though the situation you desire has already come about, in other words it's already a fact.

For example, back to my ideal home idea...

I shared with you that I wanted to live in a beautiful place with lots of space and amidst nature, with magnificent views, being able to see the stars at night and expansive sunrises and sunsets. To have a beautiful traditional house or a wooden eco-house, with a nice log fire for cosy winters. It will be near the sea in an elevated position with sea views but also with lots of greenery, trees and hills close by, etc. etc.

So now to apply affirmations to that visualization I would write...

I live in a beautiful place with space and nature around.

There are magnificent views and I am able to see stars at night and expansive sunrises and sunsets which I love.

I love the house too; it's a beautiful wooden eco-house, with a nice log fire for cosy winters.

I am near the sea in an elevated position with sea views but with lots of greenery, trees and hills close by, it's wonderful.

I am very happy, confident and living the life of my dreams.

Get the idea? I'm stating my vision as though it's already here, as though it's already my reality and I'm experiencing and enjoying it. This powerful little tool raises your vibration, which may still be of your current reality, to the vibration of what you really want.

So catapult your life to the future, six months, a year, three years from now and imagine writing a letter to a friend or relative about your life and what you're enjoying about it. It's going back to using your basic childlike, innocent imagination again. Come on, I know you always wanted to star in a big movie performing the lead part!

When you are satisfied with your list, you may proceed to Step 7.

Step 7

Well done!

So up till now we've done quite a lot of deciding and visualizing what we wish to see as our chosen reality. That's very good. Now it's time to create the strategy, the plan of action, so we can bring all our dreams into everyday waking reality.

Take the next sheet of paper. In a corner at the top write "Step 7" then as the heading write:

"The Plan of Action –
bringing these goals to life!"

Review everything you wrote for Step 5, do that now.

Now we need to get completely specific about those goals. Take one goal at a time and write in this section exactly *when* you're going to action that goal and *what* exactly you are going to do for it.

So, back to my example…

I said I would start researching and considering different areas around this country or abroad. The reasons *why* were to keep my dream alive, and to begin moving in my desired direction without delay, taking whatever little steps I could each day. The main thing is that I said I would start researching. So the question is: WHEN?

Unless I pin myself down to clear steps and specific dates there is always the danger that I may just procrastinate indefinitely, in other words, keep talking about making a change and taking some new action in life but never actually doing it! It's a terrible disease that affects many, many people. Well this step *cures it.*

Get your diary out; you will need to refer to it.

For example, using my perfect house idea again...

'I know that I have some time free on Wednesday between 11am and 12.30pm so I can definitely begin making a list of possible places I already know about, that I feel may suit me. Also, I can make those two calls to the Tourist Information Offices of the two towns that I already like very much. The day after, on Friday, I can see I have an hour free in the afternoon so I will do some internet research on the areas that come up on my list of current possibilities and on Saturday morning I can spend half the morning working out the funding of my idea and current cash flow for the next six months. I may even have to use the nine step procedure for my financial situation also.'

Now it's your turn. Remember to be as specific as possible, and enjoy never being the victim of procrastination ever again!

When you are satisfied, proceed to the penultimate step, Step 8.

Step 8

The journey has been arduous and full of peril, yet you have faced your enemies and the challenges in your path with great courage. You have made excellent and very admirable progress. There are now just two steps to go.

Now would be a good time to re-read your Outcome 1.

Many times in life I have made good progress but I failed myself, slipping back many times, because I was unaware of this vitally important step. Without this step all the previous work and progress could easily be lost. It is the step of BELIEVING. Believing in yourself, your dream and your abilities to make it happen.

Take another sheet of paper. In a corner at the top write "Step 8" then, as the heading, write:

"Believe, Affirm, Expect and Give Thanks"

It does exactly what it says on the label!

It's similar to the affirmations, but with a little extra twist.

When I originally went through this process (when my life was a mess and I had reached rock bottom, you remember my story?) I knew that, as a human being, I deserved a better reality than the one I was experiencing. The statement that arose from the depths of my being which I shouted out to the universe that fateful day was:

'I DO DESERVE MY NEW LIFE AND WHAT'S MORE IT'S WELL OVERDUE!' It continued… *'I am now changing this current reality which I have already experienced for too many years, keeping me within limiting beliefs and experiences and causing me to lose so many of my loved ones. Staying the same, in this reality, for one more day is a sentence worse than hell! It's been keeping me small-minded and is no longer an option. I've had it with part time jobs, with no real prospects and not*

managing to get by. I am choosing to end this reality today, here and now! I choose never and I mean NEVER to allow myself to live like this again.'

When all this came out of me I was, if you recall, raging. What's more, I didn't just believe this, I was affirming it to the universe and the weaker me and I was expecting a better reality from that day; there was no way it was going to continue any longer.

Somehow, when you manage to connect with this kind of clarity and conviction, you can feel as though the door has been closed on the previous experience for good, the change has happened and there is no shred of doubt left in you. You can see your future clearly and you *know* you are worthy of it. Generally, when this happens, it makes me feel full of gratitude to God and the Universe; all doubt has gone, the road is clearly marked and destiny is very close and in sight. It's a wonderful experience to have. I usually feel nothing short of totally blessed, that all I can do is express my immense gratitude to *All That Is*, the Divine in life, which has brought me to this amazing point in my personal development.

After that experience I wrote:

'I face every fear, concern or obstacle head on.
I don't waste time thinking about the problem - I act and trust myself enough to simply provide the solution as soon as it's needed.
Being positive comes from doing positive actions. Confidence comes from exercising confidence. Patience comes from being patient. Trust comes from being trusting - of yourself first.
I can turn this reality around.
I can make the new seed grow out of this old shell forever - within the next 30 days.
I am completely worthy of having a life that includes joy, personal satisfaction and fulfilment, beauty, peace, purpose, inner strength, courage, abundance, affluence and love. These are basic requirements, this is not asking too much.
These are the basics of being alive. Who am I not to experience and enjoy these qualities?
All people are magnificent, so that includes me too!
I am a magnificent person and always have been whether I, or others, saw it before or not.

I and everyone else came onto this planet to have a brilliant time, the best time possible, filled with lots of amazing and wonderful experiences of life, people and being me, expressing who I am (just like a flower that blooms, holding nothing back and giving it's magnificence equally to all) all of which I can't have when I'm dead!

I am me, Michelangelo Raiano, born at this time on this planet, with these tools available and these limitations. As everything is conducted with perfection in the universe by the magnificent power of Nature, so it is right that I am here now. Therefore, I must be experiencing the best conditions possible for my growth towards expressing the highest that I can be today. Also, I am well equipped for the task, for I have it all within me right now!

I am really grateful for all the kindness I have in my life and for the support to enable me to face this now with time, energy and conviction.

I thank you with all my heart and all of my being for showing me my mission in this lifetime as well as all the steps to get there, for making me see that I am worthy of it and that I have the ability and determination to fulfil it in this life. Thank you'

Another benefit I have found with this step is that if ever I observe a little doubt, negativity or limitation entering my thoughts, the conviction and belief that has been generated from this step has the power to instantly blast away anything that isn't that. It's brilliant to watch. Now your turn!

State your BELIEFS about yourself, AFFIRM those beliefs, EXPECT your desired reality to be yours and *always* GIVE THANKS for having been shown the way forward, who you really are and what you're capable of.

When that is completed, you may proceed to the final step, Step 9.

Step 9

Take another sheet of paper. In a corner at the top write "Step 9" then as the heading write:

"PLEDGING: The Final Step
My commitment to the person
I am becoming.
My commitment to THE REAL ME"

Out of the conviction of the previous step, the final stage, which has kept me on track, is simply my commitment to follow through. I call it pledging. It's basically a solid promise of commitment to myself that I will do everything within my power to see this process through to its completion.

It's a powerful step. When I had done most of the steps during my crisis period but hadn't got round to completing Steps 8 and 9, I noticed I began doubting my vision and fear started to creep back in. On top of this, loads of thoughts began swimming around in my head again. I had lost my clarity and hope; I was waking up at 3 a.m. every morning for a week feeling really unsettled and unsure again. 'Oh, is it ever going to stop?' I asked myself. *It stopped* as soon as I had re-read all my steps and completed Steps 8 and 9. Then I felt strong and empowered again and the whole process felt complete. I could see everything before me and everything I needed to do to get there, only this time it was all backed up with the huge belief I now had in myself through my affirmations and Step 8, coupled with my commitment to make it happen no matter what!

Some of the things I came up with were...

'I pledge to knuckle down, simply accept my discomfort and unhappiness with my current lot, face what I have to and get on with it.

I pledge to complete what I set out to do now and ignore my discomfort. In fact, I will use it to make me get on with what has to be done.

I pledge to change this old reality, a part of me for far too long, which has kept me within limiting beliefs and experiences and caused me to lose too many of my loved ones. It is no more.

I pledge that staying in that reality is not an option anymore. It was a sentence worse than death and kept me living in a small-minded world. It is no longer an option for me. I am doing it now, not tomorrow or next month – NOW!

I pledge to do it for me, for my children and future generations, for friends and everyone else who will be benefiting and growing because of this.

I pledge to follow through on this, no matter what, until the desired result is achieved.

I pledge to face whatever is thrown at me including any fears, obstacles or discomfort and simply carry on until I get what I deserve and desire.

I pledge to really focus, to get up early and actually achieve as much as possible each day, allowing myself only one late night, one night out and one outing per week, thereby making the most of this situation to complete my goal and to catapult myself, my life, into a whole new future and way of being and living.

I pledge it to me. I pledge it to my family. I pledge it all those who care for me, all who have ever loved me, all who are dear to me. I pledge it to all people everywhere, the whole of society, for the betterment of the world.'

You have done well.

Go ahead now and complete the ninth and final Step of your journey.

Chapter 5

Let us summarize what has happened.

You began this process, this journey, with an awareness of some unhappiness in your life; something or some part of your experience which deep down you knew could or should be better.

By deciding to read this book and go through the nine step procedure you said you were prepared to do something about it.

You used your powers of visualization to envisage an ideal outcome and saw how good it made you feel. You then compared this vision to your current reality with the thought of everything staying the same. You saw how that made you feel too. At that point you made your first declaration to your true self by saying "No more!" to your current situation and choosing Outcome 1 as your reality.

You saw the changes you could action, followed immediately by the reasons why you had to do them. By affirming your reality, you visualized it as already here and brought it much closer to you. The next step helped you get really specific as to what you could do and by when you would do it. Step 8 strengthened your belief in yourself and the final Step 9 became your total commitment to the real you and the new life you have chosen. Brilliant!

Now that you have had your first experience with the nine steps, the following section will be more relevant and will give you some useful tips to ensure you continue to get the maximum benefit from this nine step process of self-discovery and self-improvement.

Chapter 6

You may have tools, or coping strategies, that work very well for you in different areas of your life already, which is great. This section will provide you with some further tools that you can use as well as the nine steps to help empower yourself and to help you become master of your issue or your life as a whole. You can draw on some, or all of these, at any time. I do and with excellent results. They are my toolbox. There are also some very useful additional guidelines for the nine steps themselves. These are things that I, and others, learned along the way and which will help you apply the steps more specifically to ensure that they keep working in whatever situation they are needed.

You may be unhappy about your life but are simply not able to see a newer vision for yourself. *It can happen*. One tool that can help is known as "The Wheel of Life". It is used a lot by life coaches. First draw a large circle. Then draw lines through the circle as though you were cutting a pizza into eight slices. At the end of each line (you should have eight), on the outside of the circle, write:

Home - Health - Career - Money -
Friends/Family -
Personal Growth/Spirituality -
Partner/Relationship and Recreation/Fun.

On each line, coming from the centre of the circle to the outside, mark a scale from 0 - 10.

Then all you do is gauge how you rate each of these areas in your life using the scale. So, for example, if you feel your relationship is brilliant, put a cross on the last mark near the outside of the circle representing a 10. If you feel "money" is not so good you can put a cross closer to the centre of the circle at maybe 3 or 4 or whatever you feel it is. Then when you have done this on all the eight areas of your life, join the crosses up. What shape does your life have? Is it as balanced as you thought? Which areas stand out as needing attention? This is quite a good exercise at seeing visually what area we need to look at and address.

Another tool could be to make a list of all the things that bring you joy and nourish or nurture you in some way. You remember I did this as a way of starting to get my life back together? It is also useful, like the Wheel of Life, to highlight the aspects that are important to you and to see if you need to focus on some areas of your life more than others. If that's difficult, then simply use the process of elimination and make a list of the things you definitely *don't* want in your life. They might be easier to spot and the process will open you up, get your creative juices flowing and bring new ideas to the fore.

Sometimes it is not possible to see the bigger vision of your life or the current pressing situation. It may just be that your ideal outcome at this time would be to have time just to be, space or time to take stock, to be with yourself for a few days, or months, to help you decide what it is you really would like. Then make that your Step 1 and go through the whole nine steps to that end. It will bring you to peace.

Sometimes goals change. I noticed that occasionally I had to amend some of the steps I had written, such as my goals and my desired outcome. This was because things were getting more refined and greater clarity was coming all the time as my attention was on the necessary change every day. Sometimes I even ended up with something very different from what I had at the beginning. The main point is: do not panic if things change and adjust along the process; it's fine. It just means your vision has expanded and that's a good thing. Just continue with whatever your inner self is wishing to express and let go of your first ideas if you have to so that a more expanded and newer you/outcome can come about. Work with the issues you have before you and this process of looking at yourself and your life will bring you to where you need to be.

We never stop growing and expanding; that's why we are here *and I don't mean physically*. Life is a joy! The more we can give to life, the more we can receive. The more we grow, the more we can make use of, do and appreciate. The more we can appreciate, the more beauty, joy, love, peace and fulfilment we can enjoy. *Yes*, in everyday life!

There is no rule about how you should be or how you should live - YOU ARE UNIQUE.

Always trust your intuition; it is your best friend for life.

Take time to be alone with your soul and turn off all the usual distractions.

I once knew a family who used a small room in their house as a sanctuary, a quiet room where the only rule was that it could be used only in complete silence. I thought that was a great idea.

If your home is noisy or chaotic and you find it difficult to get any space or peace even in your own room, if you have one, then make time to be alone with your soul elsewhere. This is why I enjoy time in nature.

Fill your physical space with images of what you wish to see as your reality. Cut pictures out from magazines and brochures, anything that represents the newer you and put them up everywhere so you can see them and keep them in your awareness.

When you are visualizing or affirming your ideal outcome, it's good to project into the future and imagine everything about it. How differently will you be doing things from how you do them now? How will you be feeling? Will you be more confident, proactive, expressive, trusting, joyful? Visualize as much as possible everything about that newer, bigger reality.

"If you can dream it, you can live it"
Walt Disney

What would happen if you had an important appointment on the next street to where you are now and as you started walking there you actually tripped and fell but didn't hurt yourself in any way? Would you just stay there feeling sad about it? Would you turn back?

No! You would pick yourself up and continue. And if this happened several more times I am sure you would be surprised, perhaps a little disappointed, but you would surely continue. Therefore, if a desired outcome doesn't come immediately simply pick yourself up and continue. Keep desiring, keep visualizing and keep taking whatever small steps you can each day until the new reality is yours.

Sometimes we don't get what we want, or it comes to us in a round-about way, not in the way we expected. I know, you're thinking, how can he possibly be saying this to me now when all along he's been promising a way to get everything I want? I believe that the majority of things we visualize, desire and move towards can be ours. However, the Universe, God, the "Powers Above" will always have the final say. Don't get me wrong, the Universe only wants what we want and will always bring it to us in the way that is best for us. We see what we want for ourselves from our own standpoint and our own limited perspective but the Universe sees the whole picture, all the time, so we must allow for the fact that we may occasionally miss the mark.

Avoid getting angry or upset at these times, but rather, stay centred, connect with your intuition and aim to understand what purpose there could be to the detour or delay. Sometimes the lesson is simply to strengthen patience and trust.

During my crisis period I could have easily descended into a negative spiral at any time if I had continued dwelling on the things that were *not* right in my life. I gave them no attention whatsoever once my vision was clear. Seeing my vision, my desired outcome, gave me so much joy that whenever I caught my mind slipping back into the state of the old reality, I would immediately bring it back to my bigger picture. When doubts started creeping in I simply went over all the steps again and they would blast away all negativity by their power.

Sometimes doubt comes from the outside. Watch out for "The discouragement committee". It can come in the form of our loved ones, the people closest to us, more often than not. This is simply because they see us in one way, our old way. They don't see the new vision we see for ourselves. When you explain it to them, the first thing they feel is disbelief and then, when they see you're serious about it, *they panic*. Why? It's because it affects their personal comfort zone. It means they have to look at themselves. A lot of people would rather keep things as they are, even though not perfect, than to look honestly at themselves and face up to what they may see there. It's always very difficult when this happens, but you are not responsible for how they react to your choices in life, everyone is their own responsibility. What you have within your power is how *you choose* to react.

Never allow doubt or negative self talk to take a hold in your mind. It is such a poison. As soon as you catch it in action simply pay it no attention whatsoever, immediately bring in to your mind an image, or thought, that you prefer to have and take a step towards it if you can. After a while this process becomes second nature to you and there will be no need to constantly be on the alert. Also, you won't believe how positive a person it makes you.

"Our life is what our thoughts make it"

Marcus Aurelius

Also, act as though it were impossible to fail. When you are free of self doubt all your energy can go on your goal instead and nothing can stand in your way.

Keep a list of compliments at the back of your journal; it will help you to continue believing in yourself.

Carry a note-book with you everywhere; you never know when ideas and inspirations are going to come to you. Once you've noted them you can add them to your journal or personal folder later.

Once you have completed your nine steps you may wish to rewrite them all up into your journal or type them up and keep in a personal folder. First of all, it's good to re-read everything you've written to keep you on track and, secondly, it's all in one place so you can refer to it whenever you need.

Whenever you feel you have lost your way or doubts have come and you've slipped back into old habits or a lot of thoughts are swimming around in your mind and keeping you up every night, all you have to do is re-read your nine steps, or start the process again if another issue has arisen. All your notes, by now, should be in your journal or personal folder! By the end you will have fully reconnected with your vision, your true self, and be inspired once again to continue on your path. Re-read your nine steps regularly.

Re-read this book regularly too! It will help to keep all the important points fresh in your mind.

Significantly reduce the time you and your family spend in front of the television. It's a real life and brain killer. Better still, get rid of it completely. When I was going through my crisis period, I could have easily spent hours in front of the TV to distract myself from my problems. Instead, *I sold it*, decided to spend time facing my challenges and ended up writing this book! Occasionally, when I felt I needed to "chill" a little, I simply rented or borrowed a nice film on DVD and watched it on my computer. I also reduced the time I spent seeing and calling friends as well as the time I spent on my PC surfing the net and e-mailing people. All these things gobble up your time like some sweet-faced hungry monster.

Have early nights and a good daily routine with plenty of healthy meals, exercise and periods in natural surroundings. During times of change and transition, these simple things make a huge difference and help keep us balanced, strong and nourished.

Recognize the feelings that come with being on track in life so you can spot when you are off course and can quickly do something about it. Usually people feel more energy, excitement, enthusiasm, hope and are fired up; they feel alive, they want to get up in the morning and can't wait to start the day.

If you haven't already done so, take a look at our inspiring website: **youcanbeyourself.com** – there you will find lists of the feelings that can help you distinguish whether you are on track in life or off track, together with further tools and inspirations to get you quickly back on track and to help keep you there.

Remember Step 1 on its own has the power to change things? I sometimes use it during the day even on what I call "little situations" so I'm informing the universe of my preferred outcomes with all the little events that make up a day or week; it works *and it's great*. When you do this, notice how your day flows with more peaceful efficiency. And remember to give thanks for your blessings.

So keep re-reading your nine steps and visualizing the outcome you prefer to see happen. It is not that you are living in the future and therefore not in the present. I feel it's like looking at a map of where you are heading before a journey; you're still in the present! So keep visualizing, trust that it is not too big a job for the Universe, or God, to handle and then relax about it knowing that what you desire will be the highest probable outcome. You have repeatedly given a clear message to the Universe, the giant cosmic computer and that's all it really needs to get the ball rolling.

Experiencing an emotional crisis, or depression, is not a crime. There is actually nothing wrong with these crises when they happen. It may well be a necessary part of a person's growth to have that time alone with themselves, something they have to go through which their so called "normal" everyday life doesn't allow them to have. My own experience of depression has, on many occasions, preceded periods of greatly renewed clarity, energy and direction. I feel it's like going into the dark night of the soul, that solitary place, in order to restore my truth, balance and perspective again. The only true problem is that we often tend to resist it or continue to try and fit in with what everyone else around us expects or, alternatively, we just label it as a "bad thing" in our lives. Maybe all a person needs during those periods is time to recuperate, preferably in a beautiful and uplifting place, and to be cared for till they feel more positive or whole and can face the world again. Does our society and way of life really give people enough opportunities just to BE?

These nine steps, as well as helping you to find yourself, will also help you get your life and issues in perspective. You will see the relevance of where you currently find yourself and the things you are going through. They will help you understand the underlying purpose behind the challenges you are facing thereby giving you the strength and courage to face your fears and see things through.

A final note on manifesting:

If you can conceive of a thing, imagine it, see it in your mind's eye, then, according to the laws of the Universe, it can come about and *will* if it is desired consistently then backed by action, trust and patience. It is also vitally important to relinquish your attachment to the outcome and any predetermined time scale. *This can be the hardest thing of all* but you have to let go. After being blessed with the vision of your ideal outcome or reality, and after taking whatever little steps you can each day towards your dream, no matter how badly you want to hang onto it, you then have to hand it back to the Universe whilst maintaining complete faith, unwavering patience and absolute trust that your order is being processed, is on its way and will be delivered in exactly the right package at the most perfect time for everyone and everything concerned.

Good luck!

Chapter 7

I did not create the nine steps. I really feel that they were given to me. They were the steps I had to discover and go through myself for my own growth. They were my journey of self-discovery, my path of growth and unfoldment in this life. *Yes*, I had to go out and find them and be open to their message, but they didn't come to me unaided. I was helped along the way by many souls all the time.

The help that I was given wasn't always apparent. Sometimes the lessons came when things seemed to go wrong in life. The signs and the help are everywhere, all of the time. When I finally saw the whole picture I felt humbled and totally blessed. When one finally sees the guiding hand of the Divine in all things and in all moments, one can not help feeling total gratitude and love for *everything* that comes in life, even the knocks. I say this only that you may see it in your own life too and come to trust what you know in your heart and bring it out so that not only you but all of us can delight in your magnificence.

When you are living all your dreams, you will feel like you are in Heaven. You will feel bigger than any negative event that could befall you. You will be riding a huge wave of joy, peace, gratitude and love *all* the time. You will be living life the way it was designed to be lived, and when all of us are living our dreams and the life of our dreams then what will we have created together?

A heavenly life on earth.

So be the best you can be.

What is the best you can be?

That which you already know, that which you already are!

It is sitting inside of you right now in seed form. All that little seed needs are the right conditions; a little love, a little care and it will sprout and grow and blossom automatically. The almighty force of evolution will do the rest.

What are you waiting for?

Why waste another day in doubt? Acknowledge who you are today, *right now*. In this moment you have everything.

Forget the past, let go of the future. You have this moment, it is real, it is complete.

You have everything within you. Every dream you had about yourself before your mind cast the poison of doubt upon them and made you think you were not worthy to have what you saw in your heart. Don't let it win. Dream and never stop dreaming. Everything began as someone's dream once, what you are wearing, what you are sitting on, the music you like to hear, the food on your table, the ink on this page, *everything*. Everything you have in your life right now, everything you see around you and everything you are experiencing was somebody's dream in the past. Now it's time to put your dream out there too!

What *next* would you like to see happen in your life? Write it down now. Don't wait till things are "right" in order to begin, there is no better time than the present. Don't wait for others to do things for you. Create your own reality now! You can do it. How? Simply answer the question: What next would I like?

Write every answer that comes to you straight away from the depths of your soul without thinking, before the "thinking" mind kills it with all its limitations and tries to tell you that it's not possible.

Everything is possible and *nothing* is impossible.

We all have to think differently and think beyond the usual limited thinking currently on this planet. If nobody ever did anything differently, we would still be running around with a club in our hand, grunting.

Which reminds me...

it's easy to say "If God is so great why does he, or she, allow wars on the planet?" to give one example. However, those who promote war, violence and negativity may have to take a long, hard look deep inside themselves and realize that they *can* make different choices and *can* change the current course of life for millions of people as well as themselves. There is always a way. People have to be open to change.

In fact every problem and drop of unhappiness we see in the world today is due to limited thinking.

"We want peace, but we can't have it because they just slapped our face again." The irony is perfectly clear but no one is mature enough in their thinking to take the brave way and simply stop. The childish tactic of fighting back has never worked, why not try something else?

"We need to reduce carbon dioxide emissions NOW, but we'll give our country twenty years to drop it by ten per cent". Hey I'm happy to stop all my carbon dioxide emissions today, what can I do?

"I really want that job but I don't think I'm good enough." Then work hard for the skills and qualifications, if it means so much to you, otherwise do something for which you are qualified.

"My children are being difficult teenagers; I want them to behave differently." Why not take time to get to know who *they* really are, and what *they* enjoy. That way, you are allowing them to be themselves. They'll be far happier people, they'll feel more love and gratitude towards you and you can have the joy of watching them blossom.

"We don't like those people because they have a blue spot on their nose, they wear a pink bandana and they always do things differently to us." Well, who ever stopped a red rose being red or a yellow lily being yellow? If everything was the same and everyone looked the same, wouldn't it be a very boring planet? What would we learn from one another? What would we enjoy about others and ourselves? It is the differences that make this world so beautiful. When everyone grasps this fundamental truth, we will have an end to prejudice of all kind for good. Go

beyond the outer appearance alone and connect with the real person within, it's much more enriching for both of you.

Humans can learn a lot from flowers.

So never think in limited ways.

Every advance we ever made on this planet was because someone dared to do something differently even though they may have been ridiculed or seen as a threat at the time: Christopher Columbus, The Wright brothers, Rita Parks, Martin Luther King Jr., Jesus Christ and many other great souls, some of whom are still with us today inspiring change and growth for the better. Let us have more of these stories in the newspapers and on TV please to help encourage everyone to expand their thinking and believe in themselves.

Go beyond the norm.

Go beyond your comfort zone in everything.

Be daring.

Be different.

Find your uniqueness and bring it out!

That's what made every great person great; it wasn't their hairstyle or the car they drove.

So BE YOUR TRUE SELF always.

"Divine Love, pure love, finds its delight and satisfaction in itself. There is no need for it to be appreciated or shared; it loves for the sake of loving, even as a flower that blooms. To feel this love in oneself is to possess immutable happiness"

Maharishi Mahesh Yogi

Epilogue

I confess

I was lost
but now I am found.

Thanks to this process I was given and which I fully embraced, I changed my life around.

These nine steps worked for me

and the proof…

well, it's in your hands right now!

This was my journey. It had its highs; it had its lows - some moments of great challenge and some moments that were *absolutely exquisite.*

If I had to go through it all again, would I?

Would I change any of it or do anything differently?

Yes, I would do it all again and the only thing that I would do differently would be to trust my inner voice more, *much more*, and not allow my logical, "thinking" mind to talk me out of things.

"Know thyself"
Jesus

Thank you for sharing this journey with me.

May this nine step process and book inspire you, as it did me, to live life the way you've always imagined it could be.

Wishing you wisdom, peace, hope, joy and light always

Michelangelo

Acknowledgements

I would like to begin by giving thanks to *All That Is* - that Universal Intelligence behind all things, the Divine in life - otherwise know as God, and to some special souls who have helped me on my spiritual path.

Thank you to Maharishi Mahesh Yogi for showing me a way of bringing peace to the mind and body through the simple technique of Transcendental Meditation. Thank you for all your words of wisdom and for helping me understand myself and this journey of life much more. Thank you to all the great teachers of Truth who have ever walked this Earth, those who are with us now and those yet to come.

Thank you to my parents: Guido and Anna who have always been some of my best teachers in this lifetime just by innocently being themselves. To my children Sophia and Gabriel, two very real angels, who never fail to inspire me to be my best. To Diana Leighton who brought me my two children and showed me many areas in which I needed to grow, thank you. To my dear sister,

Helen, who has always cared for me even though at times struggled to understand my ways. Then to some of my dear friends (in no particular order): Olu and Greg Ekata, and their family, for their embodiment of the beauty of life and love; to Philip Lamba for his enthusiasm and spark for life, and his great humour; to Linda Bamber for her sincerity and goodness; to Peter Reynolds, the constant rock of inner wisdom and truth who never fails to amaze me with his unexpected nougats of practical wisdom; to Veronique Raingeval for her clarity of perception and intuition, together with the love in her heart for life and people; to Cathy Macbeth for her friendship and her ability to always keep optimistic in the face of life's adversities; to Birte Glüsing, an unassuming knower of truth and very encouraging friend; to Robert Johnstone, supportive friend in the face of life's practicalities and for his inspiring ability to make the most of life regardless of its challenges; to Helen Evans for her compassionate heart and for completing the initial editing on this book. Finally, I thank the many other great souls who have blessed me with their gifts at some point in my life, and to the ones I am yet to meet.

I love you and thank you all

Lord, make me an instrument of your peace.
Where there is hatred, let me sow love;
where there is injury, pardon;
where there is doubt, faith;
where there is darkness, light;
where there is despair, hope;
and where there is sadness, joy.
Divine Master, grant that I may not so
much seek to be consoled as to console,
to be understood as to understand,
to be loved as to love.
For it is in giving that we receive,
it is in pardoning that we are pardoned,
and in dying that we are born to eternal life.

St. Francis of Assisi

Keep in touch!

Register for my free e-newsletter online and
also do let me know of your experiences with
this book and the 9 Step Process.

I'd love to hear from you.

Michelangelo

See you soon at

youcanbeyourself.com